Portfolio, Programme and Project Offices Pocketbook

Published by TSO (The Stationery Office)
and available from:

Online
www.tsoshop.co.uk
Mail, Telephone, Fax & E-mail
TSO
PO Box 29, Norwich, NR3 1GN
Telephone orders/General enquiries:
0870 600 5522
Fax orders: 0870 600 5533
E-mail: customer.services@tso.co.uk
Textphone 0870 240 3701
TSO@Blackwell and other Accredited Agents

ISBN 9780113314454 (Sold in a pack of 10 copies)
ISBN 9780113314430 (Single copy ISBN)

Printed in the United Kingdom for The Stationery Office

Material is FSC certified. Sourced from responsible sources.

Contents

Acknowledgements

AXELOS acknowledges with thanks the contribution of Eileen Roden (QA) in the construction of this pocketbook.

In addition, AXELOS would like to recognize the contribution of Sue Taylor (P3O chief examiner) and Sue Vowler (Project Angels Ltd, mentor for the 2013 edition of P3O) who acted as reviewers.

1 Introduction

The right P3O® (Portfolio, Programme and Project Offices) model will provide a focal point for defining a balanced portfolio of change and ensuring consistent delivery of programmes and projects across an organization or department. It could successfully take many forms, from a single all-encompassing physical office to a virtual office model made up of a permanent organization portfolio office supported by a permanent hub portfolio office or temporary programme/project offices.

The purpose of this pocketbook is to introduce the principles, processes and techniques that will enable individuals and organizations to successfully establish, develop and maintain (or in some cases re-energize) appropriate support structures that will facilitate:

- Informing senior management's decision-making on prioritization, risk management, deployment of resources etc. across the organization to successfully deliver their business objectives (portfolio management)
- Delivery of programmes and projects within time, cost and quality constraints
- Identification and realization of outcomes and benefits via programmes and projects.

The publication describes a structured approach to identifying the goals and scope of a P3O, along with the requisite functions and services. It also provides an implementation lifecycle that ensures the organization's P3O goals are affordable, add value, and are delivered in an effective and efficient manner.

1.1 PORTFOLIO, PROGRAMME AND PROJECT MANAGEMENT ENVIRONMENT

Many organizations operate in a complex environment, with multiple programmes and projects being delivered at any one time.

1.1.1 What is a portfolio?

Definition: portfolio

The totality of an organization's investment (or segment thereof) in the changes required to achieve its strategic objectives.

Definition: portfolio management

A coordinated collection of strategic processes and decisions that together enable the most effective balance of organizational change and business as usual.

The focus of portfolio management is delivery of the organization's strategy. It achieves this by ensuring that:

- Changes to business as usual are agreed at the appropriate management level and contribute to at least one strategic objective
- Strategic decisions are based on a clear understanding of cost, risk, impact on business as usual and the strategic benefit to be realized
- Resources and changes are prioritized in line with the current environment, existing changes, resource capacity and capability
- All changes are reviewed frequently in terms of progress, cost, risk priority, benefits and strategic alignment.

Portfolio management aligns the delivery of programmes and projects with strategic objectives, business requirements and the organization's capability, its capacity for change and its portfolio, programme and project management (PPM) maturity. Portfolio management is an active and iterative process that requires the collection and analysis of timely, accurate and relevant information about the organization's investment initiatives (programmes and projects) in one place – providing one version of the truth.

Portfolio management should consider not just those programme and project commitments comprising the organization's change agenda, in terms of resources (i.e. money, people, infrastructure and other facilities), but should also consider the wider business picture, taking account of business as usual. Only by understanding and appreciating the organization's full suite of commitments, i.e. corporate, programme, project and business as usual, can a fully balanced business portfolio be achieved.

In practice, portfolio management is carried out at many different levels in an organization: at corporate, directorate, divisional or even departmental level.

1.1.2 What is a programme?

Definition: programme

A temporary, flexible organization structure created to coordinate, direct and oversee the implementation of a set of related projects and activities in order to deliver outcomes and benefits related to the organization's strategic objectives. A programme is likely to have a life that spans several years.

Managing Successful Programmes (MSP®) should be referred to for detailed guidance on the management of programmes.

1.1.3 What is a project?

Definition: project

A temporary organization that is created for the purpose of delivering one or more business products according to an agreed business case.

Managing Successful Projects with PRINCE2® should be referred to for detailed guidance on the management of projects.

1.2 P3O AND PORTFOLIO, PROGRAMME AND PROJECT LIFECYCLES

The P3O model may comprise portfolio, programme and project offices, all of which may add value at different stages of the portfolio, programme or project lifecycles (see Figure 1.1).

Figure 1.1 P3O model elements aligned with portfolio, programme and project lifecycles

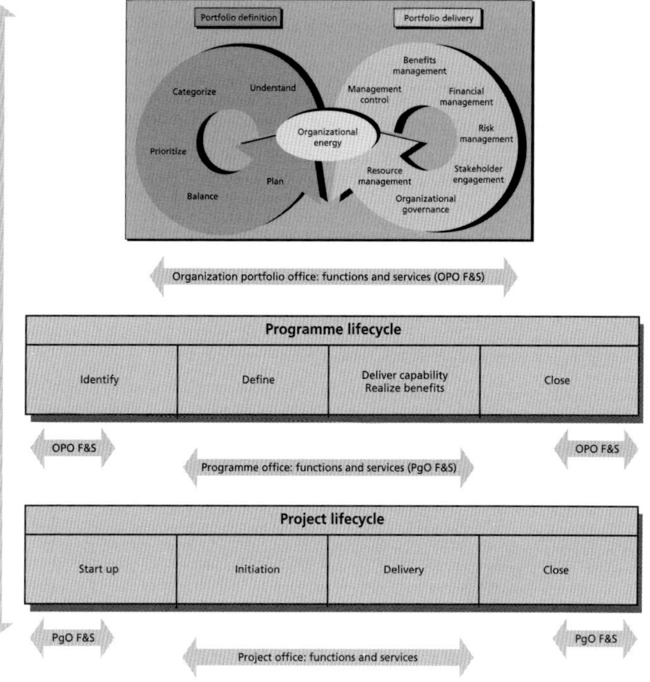

2 What are P3Os?

Definition: Portfolio, Programme and Project Offices (P3O)

The decision-enabling and support business model for all business change within an organization. This will include single or multiple physical or virtual structures, i.e. offices (permanent and/or temporary), providing a mix of central and localized functions and services, and integration with governance arrangements and the wider business such as other corporate support functions.

2.1 ROLE AND FOCUS OF A P3O

The phrases 'doing the right programmes and projects' and 'doing programmes and projects right' are often used to describe the role of a P3O or one of the individual offices within the P3O. It is important to understand the differences between the two:

- **Doing the right programmes and projects** Describes the need to ensure that business investment is spent on the things that matter and that the focus is on delivering programmes and projects that enable achievement of the corporate strategy.
- **Doing programmes and projects right** Describes the need to deliver programmes and projects consistently and well.

This can be expanded as shown in Figure 2.1.

5 Roles within a P3O model

When designing the P3O and deciding on the right model, job descriptions should be identified that are specific for each resource. The job descriptions may focus on a management role (e.g. head of programme office), a generic role (e.g. portfolio analyst), a specific function (e.g. finance officer) or a combination of different functions.

Outlines of the various roles are provided in the following sections. The role descriptions can be treated as a 'pick and mix' set to create customized job descriptions tailored to the organization's business and customer requirements.

5.1 MANAGEMENT ROLES

P3O sponsor

The P3O sponsor is a senior manager who directs and champions the establishment and evolving operation of the P3O. They will ideally be a member of the main board.

Head of P3O (permanent office)

The head of P3O (also known as head of portfolio office) establishes and runs the office.

This role requires strong leadership and management skills, coupled with strong PPM or strategy/business-planning skills, to ensure the integrity of the portfolio or programmes and projects. The individual will also provide strategic challenge, overview and scrutiny, ensuring alignment with wider policy and strategic initiatives.

After closing the programme, it is essential to maintain the role of P3O sponsor as a champion for the P3O and maintain relationships with the key stakeholders. The P3O needs to continue to provide functions and services that are aligned with the business requirements, and it is likely that support and investment will be required for further changes to be delivered through subsequent programmes or projects.

Figure 2.2 An example of a P3O model

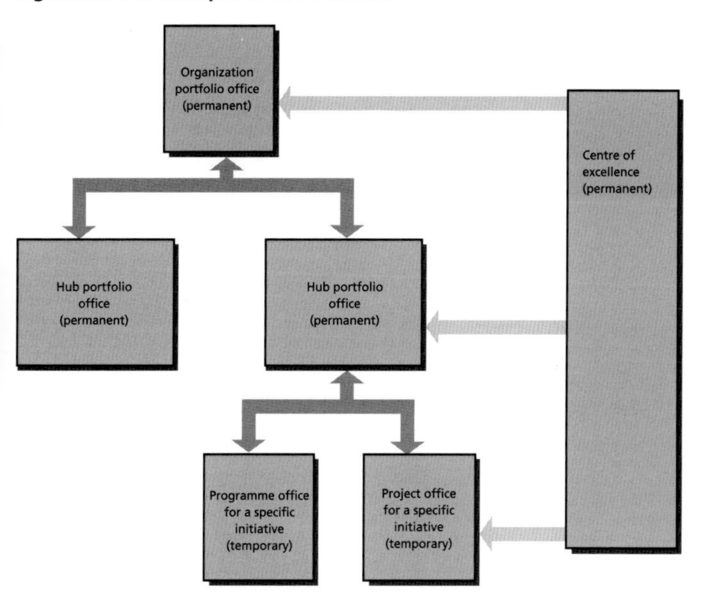

The portfolio office will be responsible for advising senior management on the composition of the portfolio, its progress against plans and any conflicting priorities (including impacts on business operations), risks and issues. The senior management board may have to make hard choices about programmes, projects and resources in the light of changing priorities. It therefore requires the portfolio office to provide the challenge and scrutiny of portfolio information and recommend options/ decisions to support those choices.

Table 2.1 P3O model elements

Element	P3O context
Organization portfolio office	A permanent office set up to support the definition and delivery of a portfolio of change across the entire organization or enterprise
Hub portfolio office	A permanent office set up to support the definition and delivery of a portfolio of programmes and projects within a department, division, geographical region or business unit
Programme office	A temporary office set up to support the delivery of a specific change initiative being delivered as a programme
Project office	A temporary office set up to support the delivery of a specific change initiative being delivered as a project
Centre of excellence (COE)	A portfolio, programme and project management standards office, which defines standards (processes, templates and tools), skills and training, manages knowledge and may provide independent assurance. The COE may be part of a portfolio office or exist as a separate independent office

A typical portfolio office provides the means to:

- Establish a structure for selecting the right programmes and projects for the organization
- Ensure the ongoing alignment of programmes and projects with strategic objectives and targets
- Assess whether new requirements can be accommodated within existing organizational capability, capacity and maturity
- Allocate the right resources to the right programmes and projects
- Ensure scrutiny and challenge
- Identify and manage dependencies between programmes and projects
- Resolve conflicts and contentions for scarce and costly resources (these could be technical or business resources as well as change resources)
- Assist with the identification of threats and opportunities, and evaluate the true implications of the aggregate level of programme and project risk
- Monitor the progress of programmes and projects against key objectives
- Ensure the ongoing successful delivery of programmes and projects
- Adopt value management – active management of the portfolio to optimize value, realize benefits and feed back learning into the investment selection and portfolio prioritization process
- Achieve value-for-money savings and efficiency gains from programme and project rationalization
- Ensure the organization has a balanced portfolio, with consideration given to the ability of the organization to absorb change with the least disruption to business as usual

- Link change benefits to the performance management structure
- Ensure investment in research and development activities for the long-term survival of the organization.

Although the key role of a portfolio office is identified as ensuring that the 'right' things are delivered, there is also a requirement to ensure that change is delivered consistently and well, through standard processes and trained, competent staff. This consistency of delivery is often provided by a COE, which provides standards, consistency of methods and processes, knowledge management, assurance and training across the full portfolio of change. The COE may be a team or function within the organization portfolio office or may be set up as a separate office. When a new programme or project is established, the COE is the first place to go to get methods, tools, training or advice, and to seek guidance on any lessons learned from previous similar changes. Similarly, throughout, and at the end of the programme or project, any lessons learned should go back to the COE so that they can be passed on to future teams. In this way, the organization rises up the maturity curve for programmes and projects.

When a specific change initiative is launched as a programme or project, it may require its own temporary programme or project office. This may be resourced from an organization-wide permanent portfolio office or a local hub portfolio office (based on business units, divisions, departments or geographic regions), providing resources and standards for the life of the programme or project. The temporary project or programme office may support the project or programme manager and relevant board with planning, risk management, issue resolution and change management, or act as information librarian. On small projects, the support may simply be provided by a multitasking project support officer.

2.3 FACTORS INFLUENCING P3O MODEL DESIGN

Factors including the organization's size, physical structure, governance structures, resourcing policies and maturity will all play a part in:

- What kind of P3O model should be deployed
- How many separate offices there should be
- What functions and services the offices provide
- Where the component offices are physically located.

The following design considerations are relevant for a single office or multiple offices:

- **Reporting lines** A P3O is often made up of multiple offices, each serving a particular business need. However, for the P3O model to add maximum value to an organization, it should ultimately report to a main board director, preferably the strategy or business change director. If the P3O model is to provide support to the organization's governance for all change programmes and projects, its final point of escalation for decisions, priorities, risks, issues and changes should be the main board.

  Where an organization portfolio office exists, it should report directly to a main board director, the chief executive officer (CEO), chief operating officer (COO), chief financial officer (CFO) or chief information officer (CIO). If the portfolio office is a hub portfolio office in a decentralized model, aligned with a division or department, it should report to the divisional director or most senior role within the department.

Where a COE exists (in a separate office from the portfolio office), it often reports to a corporate services function or directorate, aligned with other cross-organizational standards and assurance departments such as audit, finance, procurement or communications.

Reporting lines should also be considered at programme and project office level. Should the office be self-contained within the programme or project, with direct reporting lines to the programme or project manager? Could the services be provided more effectively by a programme office or hub portfolio office reporting to a programme manager or projects director, with the same services being provided to several projects?

- **Centralized versus decentralized offices** In a centralized P3O model, there may be a single P3O office, sitting in a central corporate function or department, that will perform one or all of the portfolio support, delivery and COE functions. Alternatively, there may be a number of central offices set up, each specifically addressing portfolio support, delivery or COE functions. In large organizations or functionally focused organizations, with decentralized decision-making and a policy of deploying local resources closest to business delivery, a partially or fully decentralized model may be more appropriate. A small central office with portfolio support and COE functions can be supplemented with delivery functions and local portfolio and COE functions operating out of hub portfolio offices. Decentralized models focus support on local need, but care must be taken to ensure adherence to a consistent organization-wide set of standards, albeit with local variations.
- **Permanent versus temporary offices** A P3O can consist of permanent offices, temporary offices or a combination of both.

It is recommended that permanent offices are established to provide functions and services that support ongoing portfolios, senior management decision-making and the setting of generic standards for all change initiatives. These are likely to be organization portfolio offices, local hub portfolio offices and COEs, resourced by permanent staff trained to perform specific functions. In some permanent offices there may be a core of permanent staff supplemented by contract staff to meet peaks and troughs of workload or to provide an input of expertise to develop new standards etc.

When a new programme or project is launched, it may require its own temporary programme or project office. If there is a permanent office (portfolio office or hub portfolio office) with a central flexible delivery team, resources may be requested from there. However, in some organizations the central pool may not exist or may not be big enough to cope with demand, in which case business staff may be seconded to project roles with support from a COE, or contract staff may be engaged.

- **Co-located versus distributed models** The ideal scenario is to have a permanent organization office with staff physically co-located, ensuring team cohesion and consistency of approach. However, in some organizations a distributed model exists because of a lack of physical office space, adherence to work/life-balance policies that allow individuals to work near their homes, or the location of functional experts with other teams. Where a distributed office exists, it is essential that there is an acknowledged single set of standards, albeit with separate owners for components of the standards. It is also vital that the distributed team communicates often and well, through the use of meetings, central information portals and collaborative working practices.

3 What should the P3O do?

3.1 FUNCTIONS AND SERVICES WITHIN A P3O MODEL

There are many functions and services that the P3O can provide. Those provided should contribute directly to the outcomes required by the organization and should be based on the business drivers, levels of governance and customer demands. Although every office may deliver all of the functions and services, each office may have a specific functional emphasis – planning, delivery or centre of excellence (COE). The focus for each functional area is shown in Figure 3.1.

Organization portfolio offices primarily focus on strategic planning/portfolio support services, whereas temporary programme and project offices focus on delivery support services. COE services may be provided by a separate office or may be integrated into portfolio, programme or project offices (see example in Figure 3.2). The key driver is 'adding value at the point of service delivery'.

Some functions and services exist only at portfolio level, whereas others may exist at portfolio, programme and project level but have different input/support requirements. An example of how the function of risk management may be delivered through services within the various functional areas is detailed below:

- Within the **strategic planning/portfolio support** functional area, risk is considered from a strategic viewpoint, looking at risks that may inhibit the organization's ability to deliver its strategic objectives and opportunities to exceed them.

Figure 3.1 High-level functions and services of a P3O model

P3O	Planning (portfolio)	Portfolio build, prioritization, analysis and reporting
		Programme and project set-up and closure
		Stakeholder engagement and communications
		Planning and estimating
		Capacity planning and resource management
		Benefits management
		Performance monitoring
	Delivery (programme and project)	Planning and estimating
		Monitor and review
		Reporting
		Risk management
		Issue management
		Change control
		Finance
		Commercial (including supplier management)
		Quality assurance
		Information management (including configuration and asset management)
		Transition management
		Secretariat
	Centre of excellence	Standards and methods (processes and tools)
		Internal consultancy
		Organizational learning and knowledge management
		People and skills (PPM competencies)

Figure 3.2 An example of a P3O model with key functions

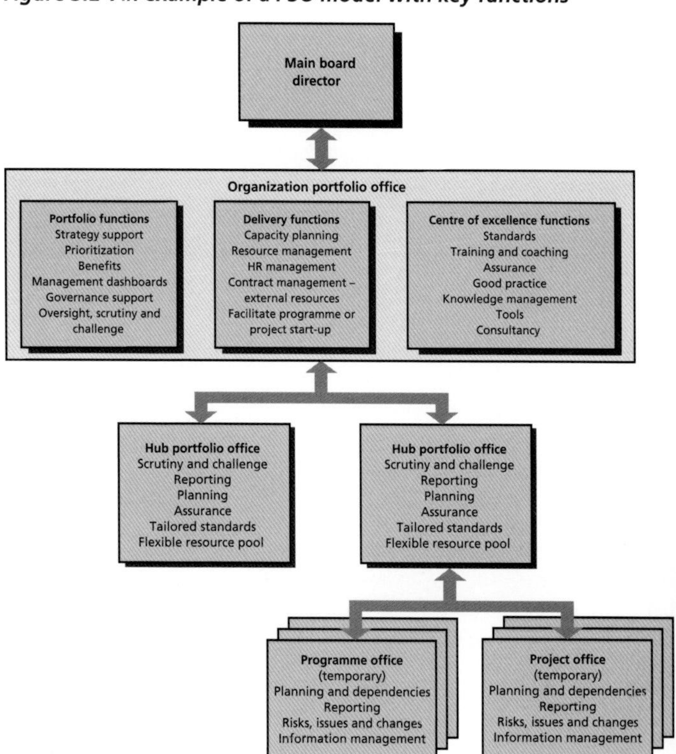

- Within the **delivery support** functional area, programme-level risk is considered with regard to the ability to achieve the planned outcomes and benefits for a specific business change. At project level, risk is considered with regard to the delivery of the project's outputs to meet the required objectives on time, cost, benefits, quality and scope.
- Within the **centre of excellence** functional area, the P3O should provide a standard risk management strategy, process and templates to ensure consistent application of risk management and standardized risk registers.

3.2 P3O ASSURANCE FUNCTIONS AND SERVICES

Independent assurance services are often provided by an office within the P3O. The services may take many forms, such as coordinating or facilitating gated reviews (in UK government, the OGC Gateway™), regular health checks, internal or external audits, or learning reviews.

Assurance teams may also offer quality assurance services to programmes and projects, by providing an assurance resource (full- or part-time) or independent advice/guidance on the tailoring of processes in the start-up stage.

Whatever the level of assurance service provided, it is essential that it is independent of the programme or project delivery and that there are no conflicts of interest.

The P3O itself should also be subject to independent assurance and external audit, in particular the external review of COE functions and services, to ensure that good practice is being kept up to date with changing industry standards and trends.

Within a multi-programme/project environment, staff across the P3O may carry out assurance at appropriate checkpoints and at gated reviews, as well as providing ongoing oversight, scrutiny and challenge. Independent assurance external to the delegated assurance from the programme or project board may be requested by senior management boards and may be focused on fulfilment of strategy, impact on business operations, management of dependencies or other areas of concern.

3.3 P3O GOVERNANCE FUNCTIONS AND SERVICES

The P3O model seeks to provide the governance backbone for all change within an organization, ensuring that all decisions are made at the appropriate level, with accurate information in a timely manner. This means that the P3O needs to work effectively with all bodies across the organization that either make decisions or provide facts and information to allow a decision to be made. The PPM governance cannot be developed in isolation from the business-as-usual decision-making bodies. The relationship between the P3O and these bodies should be defined and rules of engagement established.

Governance must be agreed and defined in terms of:

- Who makes what decision and when
- What delegated limits of authority are in place
- The rules and routes for escalation and cascading of information, risks, issues and changes.

The agreement should reflect the governance and information needs of all stakeholders.

The terms of reference for all the offices within the P3O should detail their specific governance responsibilities.

4 How to implement or re-energize a P3O

4.1 P3O LIFECYCLE

As the implementation or re-energizing of a P3O is likely to create a significant level of business change (including the need to change mindsets and behaviours), it is recommended that the implementation or re-energizing of the P3O is managed as a programme using *Managing Successful Programmes* (MSP), with:

- A defined budget, expected outcomes and timescales to delivery
- Appropriate governance, including a P3O sponsor to act as project executive or senior responsible owner (SRO) for the programme
- Adherence to an appropriate lifecycle and processes.

However, it is recognized that in some organizations, programme management may not yet have been adopted or the change may be limited to a simple office set-up or introduction of a new system or service. In this case the P3O design and implementation may be managed as a project. In small organizations where the P3O unit is simply one or two individuals, the P3O implementation may be managed as a series of incremental business changes, delivered as part of business as usual.

In some organizations, where there is insufficient stakeholder buy-in for a programme or project, the initial formation of the P3O and early improvements are often delivered with an evolutionary approach, using small incremental business changes delivered by a P3O enthusiast. Without appropriate funding and buy-in, the services provided will be of limited scope. Effort must be focused on building credibility through the value of the services provided in order to gain the required investment in time and money to design and deliver an appropriate model for the organization.

Whatever the approach taken, it is important to have a good understanding of the problems that are intended to be solved or the opportunities to be maximized, supported by a vision of the future P3O provision and a time-phased plan to achieve that vision. It is also important to engage effectively with stakeholders, communicate well and keep a focused eye on benefits. Even if the P3O model is being implemented as a project or business-as-usual change, some elements of MSP are well worth incorporating, including the vision statement, blueprint, benefits management, and leadership and stakeholder engagement.

Introducing a P3O model can be a major cultural change, and it may be necessary to implement it in several steps or tranches. Each step must deliver real benefits, ideally at all levels of management, first to gain buy-in and later to sustain it. The typical implementation lifecycle for a permanent P3O is shown in Figure 4.1.

Figure 4.1 Implementation lifecycle for a permanent P3O model

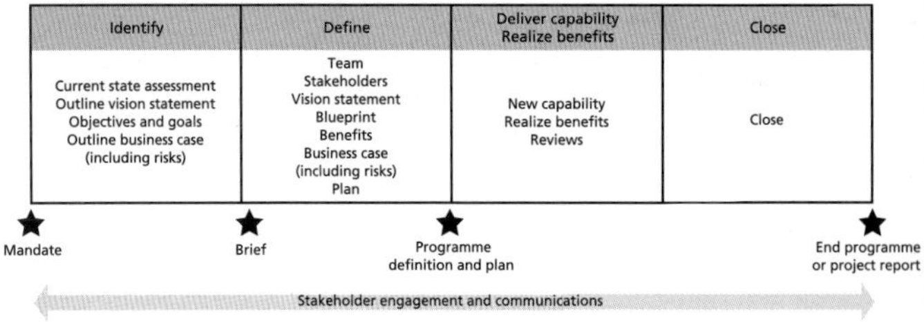

Identify	Define	Deliver capability Realize benefits	Close
Current state assessment Outline vision statement Objectives and goals Outline business case (including risks)	Team Stakeholders Vision statement Blueprint Benefits Business case (including risks) Plan	New capability Realize benefits Reviews	Close

4.2 IDENTIFY

4.2.1 Current state assessment

As in all change programmes, success requires: an understanding of the problems that need to be solved and the opportunities that need to be maximized; recognition of the need for change; and commitment and consensus on how the change will be delivered.

Senior managers need to be asked which issues and problems they rate as critical. Consensus is required, preferably at the main board level. This ensures that the P3O sponsor understands what success looks like across the organization from differing viewpoints and allows them to gain consensus on a common P3O vision. Gathering these views and gaining consensus may take the form of a series of interviews, workshops or surveys focusing on recent issues or reviews, such as:

- We recently undertook a portfolio review and 48% of projects are currently at red-light status in the corporate risk register.
- We are currently investing in training, tools and methods; however, our programme outcomes are not where we want them to be. Should we consider a more structured approach to P3O investment?
- Investment in an enterprise PPM tool is being planned. What enterprise business model will need to be in place to integrate with this tool to ensure that we achieve the business value from the investment?
- The current P3O is no longer meeting our needs and we need to re-energize it to add value.
- A P3M3® capability assessment was undertaken and our next key competency is to achieve an organizational focus. How might this be applied in our organization?

- We have recently aligned our existing portfolio of projects and programmes with the strategic objectives of our organization, and the initial findings are that 27% of our current changes do not support the strategic objectives.
- Project start-ups always take considerable time and effort to determine the 'new' standards to be used.
- Too much is going over time; too much is going over budget; we are doing too much at the same time.

Very few 'best-in-class' P3Os appear overnight in a green-field site; an organization often has existing programme or project offices carrying out some, if not all, of the services required by the ideal model. Therefore, in order to create a vision of what the P3O should be providing, it is necessary to understand what is being offered now and how effective it is. Typical questions to ask during data gathering are:

- Is the existing P3O doing the right things?
- What is the current perception from stakeholders – is it favourable, and why?
- Are they doing what they do well?
- Do we have the right people and skills with the correct level of seniority and authority to get things done?
- What should the P3O stop doing?
- What should the P3O start doing?
- How are 'best-in-class' P3Os operating in similar industries or sectors?

4.2.2 Outline vision statement

Once it has been agreed what problems the organization is trying to solve and how a P3O could help, the next step is to develop an outline vision statement for the P3O. This should be a clear vision of what the organization's new business model will be, and how success will be measured, with a clear link to the business strategy showing how these changes will contribute to the organization's key objectives.

The outline vision statement will be supported by the first iteration of the blueprint, defining what the new or revised P3O model will look like in terms of organization and services – a picture of the desired future state.

The blueprint of the future P3O model should also consider how the P3O will enable the delivery of organization-wide business processes. The P3O may own some business processes or contribute to processes owned by other business functions. A key success factor in developing a P3O model is to understand what processes the P3O can and cannot influence. Where a business process is owned by another function, e.g. finance, the P3O should understand how to interface with it effectively.

4.2.3 Objectives and goals

The objectives and goals for the new or re-energized P3O need to be agreed by the various stakeholders. These may be at portfolio, programme or project level. There should be clear alignment between the new capability being delivered and the outcomes required.

4.2.4 Outline business case (including risks)

Like any investment decision, implementation of the P3O model, whether by programme, project or incremental business changes, should have a formally agreed business case. The purpose of the business case is to clearly identify the plan, benefits and risks involved with the implementation of the P3O model. As with every business case, it should answer the questions often asked by senior management: 'Why have any form of P3O?' and 'What value does it add to our investment portfolio?'

4.3 DEFINE

The key activities within the Define process are as follows:

1. Team – establish the implementation team
2. Stakeholders – identify and analyse stakeholders
3. Vision statement – refine the vision statement
4. Blueprint – develop the P3O blueprint
5. Benefits – develop, model and validate the benefits
6. Business case (including risks) – develop the business case, risk register and risk management strategy
7. Plan – identify stages/tranches of delivery and develop the implementation or transition plan.

These activities are not sequential and often happen in parallel. All definition activities are scalable, and for a small organization or small P3O operation, the approach should be tailored to suit local need and available resources.

4.3.1 Define activity 1 – Establish the implementation team

It is critical that the implementation team has the right mix of skills and experience (or has access to them) to ensure that a pragmatic P3O model is defined and implemented. Fundamentally, a core team with capabilities in strategic and business analysis, and portfolio, programme and project management is required, with associated specialist knowledge of processes, tools and techniques.

The members of the team set up to establish or transform the P3O may also be the individuals who will form the core team working within the operational P3O going forward, or they may be a mix of long-term staff and interim resources. Particular care should be taken in the choice of programme manager. There should be clear separation from the P3O sponsor (who will take the role of project executive or SRO for the programme). Where the programme manager will take on the role of head of P3O, or head of a programme or project office, independent assurance should be engaged to validate the design of the P3O.

4.3.2 Define activity 2 – Identify and analyse stakeholders

As with any change programme that affects multiple stakeholders, it is essential to understand who the members of the stakeholder community are, who will be affected or impacted by the changes, who will be winners and who may be losers. Thus:

- Carry out a stakeholder analysis of all those involved in or impacted by the P3O model development or improvement programme. This will include senior managers, business unit managers, the programme and project management delivery community, P3O staff (old and new), external suppliers and business process owners of linked units.
- A key success factor is to enthuse a champion (P3O sponsor) – a senior manager with authority, influence and charisma. This should be someone who can engage with the organization at all levels, particularly at senior manager level, to sell the P3O vision, engender commitment and obtain the necessary investment funds.

- Develop an effective communication plan to educate stakeholders in the value of the P3O, make them aware of the services the P3O will or does offer, and engage their commitment for the new world that will follow the P3O model roll-out.
- Do not just communicate what is being done (or could be done): develop a marketing plan for the P3O; develop a 'brand' and a slogan or strap line; use 'selling tactics'; advertise successes (using facts and numbers); and use case studies, leaflets and posters to announce what the P3O does and has achieved. Use all available media, particularly intranets, portals, internal newspapers and team briefings, to get the message across.
- Finally, don't just communicate once – use regular programme/project management forums to share lessons, coach people in new approaches, tools and techniques, and make the P3O the first port of call when an issue arises.

4.3.3 Define activity 3 – Refine the vision statement

Ensure that the outline vision statement developed during the Identify process is refined to include a high-level view of the outcomes that will be achieved across process, organizational, technology and information areas once the programme is completed. This will be a critical marketing tool to communicate the goals of the programme across the wider organization and build momentum, as a significant number of staff may be impacted.

4.3.4 Define activity 4 – Develop the P3O blueprint

The blueprint will describe the future state of the P3O, to be met either in a single tranche of delivery or through multiple tranches (along with an intermediate blueprint for each tranche). It should include sections on:

1. Processes (including operational costs and performance levels)
2. Organizational structure
3. Technology (including tools and techniques)
4. Information and data requirements.

Blueprint section 1 – Processes (including operational costs and performance levels)

Define and agree which functions and services will be required to address the issues being faced and to meet future expectations of the P3O. Consider using pictures, process models or swimlanes to demonstrate processes, interfaces, roles and responsibilities. The attention of senior managers and other users of the P3O is more likely to be gained if the key processes defined within the P3O model can be described on a single page.

Blueprint section 2 – Organizational structure

The underlying goal in establishing an organization-wide P3O is to bring structure to decision-making and business change practices across an organization, with a clear line of sight from strategic goals down to local change decisions and working practices. In designing the P3O model, a key outcome will be a joined-up governance model that enables a clear strategic understanding of priorities, progress, key risks and issues, thereby enabling confident decision-making with points of accountability at all levels.

Once it has been agreed where the component offices of the P3O model will sit, where they will report to and whom they will serve in terms of customers, the P3O model itself should be designed in terms of reporting lines, structure, roles and responsibilities.

The functions and services that are owned by the P3O, or that the P3O contributes to at portfolio, programme or project level, will drive the role types, the organizational components and the number of staff required to operate the P3O functions and services. See Chapter 5 for outline roles and responsibilities.

When building the P3O staffing plan, first define the staff skills profiles, then assess the current staff (if a P3O exists) or available staff, and define an action or development plan to fill any gaps. Consider options for training, mentoring or coaching for existing or new staff. Buy in short-term help to fast-track start-up. Finally, don't neglect qualifications for staff within the P3O, to give credibility to the people and the services they provide.

Blueprint section 3 – Technology (including tools and techniques)

It is critical to match the PPM maturity of the organization with the sophistication of the tools and technologies to be employed in achieving pragmatic solutions. It may be that a manual process is more appropriate at the outset than an automated process or tools.

Tools and technologies should not necessarily be limited to schedule management or planning-and-control-related software. Consideration should also be given to the level of integration to limit or remove data duplication at the programme or project manager and team level, such as a single risk management tool that can filter for team, project or programme.

Blueprint section 4 – Information and data requirements

The blueprint will detail all the data requirements of the P3O to support the various functions and services to be provided. Careful consideration must be given to information assurance and the additional costs that appropriate controls and processes will incur.

It is also important to document the proposed reporting requirements for the future-state P3O. This will need to integrate with the organizational component of the blueprint and align with the requirements of:

- Governance groups, e.g. senior management board, divisional boards, programme and project boards, and steering groups
- Components within the P3O, e.g. between portfolio, programme and project offices
- Programme and project delivery groups
- Corporate support functions, e.g. finance, audit, quality, procurement, marketing and communications
- Benefit owners, business change managers and business change teams
- External groups (if required).

The blueprint should also describe the need for alignment with the principle of management by exception and the use of highlight and exception-based reporting.

4.3.5 Define activity 5 – Develop, model and validate the benefits

It is essential to focus on the benefits the P3O will deliver and formally track the realization of these over time. Develop a benefits management strategy, benefits map, benefit profiles and benefits realization plan.

In creating benefit profiles and developing the benefits management strategy, there are significant opportunities to generate commitment and support for the P3O concept and its value to the organization.

Some of the benefit drivers (translatable into benefit profiles) that a P3O may provide are:

- **Increased cost savings** Delivering the same capabilities with less business change investment
- **Increased strategic alignment** Reducing investment in programmes and projects that only provide tactical value to the business goals of the organization
- **More effective use of resources** Less non-productive time for resources and/or a reduction in the reliance on external resources in the delivery of new capabilities.

4.3.6 Define activity 6 – Develop and confirm the business case (including risks)

At this stage in the lifecycle, more detailed information becomes available and, as the blueprint develops, the business case should continue to be revised and refined throughout the Define stage. Detailed costings for the resources and tools required to deliver the agreed functions and services will be more accurate and, along with the proposed implementation plan, a baseline cash flow can be developed.

As with any other programme, it is necessary to document how risks will be managed and communicated.

4.3.7 Define activity 7 – Plan stages or tranches of delivery

Each P3O model implementation or re-energization will have its own unique combination and phasing of initiatives to achieve the future-state business model (as defined in the blueprint). It is important to adopt an incremental approach to reduce the adverse impacts of a 'big bang' implementation and to demonstrate benefits to senior management from the investment in the P3O.

Design the implementation or re-energization plan so that the first tranche of delivery contains early critical improvement. Go for early benefits that achieve demonstrable improvements, and consider those deliverables that are simple to implement, are visible to senior management and increase the credibility of the P3O. For example, create a portfolio register – a list of all programmes and projects being undertaken by the organization, their link to strategy, value, key stakeholders and delivery timeframe. For the first time, the senior management team will be able to see all changes in the organization. Following on from that, carry out a rationalization exercise to identify duplications of effort or initiatives that may be counterproductive. Add exception-based reporting through a management dashboard to the portfolio toolkit and senior managers will buy into the P3O's value and continued existence. The investment cash released by stopping projects that should never have started in the first place will provide funding for the subsequent tranches of P3O service roll-out.

4.4 DELIVER

Successes should be communicated regularly to all stakeholders, in particular those controlling the funding of the P3O model. Each tranche of delivery should be seen as adding value to the organization and may generate funding for subsequent tranches of delivery until the optimal solution is reached.

4.4.1 Deliver new capability, and transition and stabilize operations

Throughout delivery it is essential to develop close links with the impacted business areas to ensure the rate of change is bearable and the required level of ongoing support is maintained. The way in which new processes and tools are implemented and embedded through delivery will have a direct impact on the credibility of, and ongoing support for, the P3O.

4.4.2 Realize benefits

Benefits will be realized throughout the programme to implement the P3O model, not just post-programme.

Benefit profiles must be maintained, reflecting the benefits realized and updated with the latest view of realized and expected benefits. It is essential that delivered benefits are aligned with the programme outcomes and organization strategy, and made visible to senior management and other key stakeholders to retain their ongoing support.

4.4.3 Periodic reviews

As a minimum, a review should be undertaken at the end of each tranche/stage of delivery to ensure that lessons have been learned and they have informed the approach and plan for the subsequent tranche(s).

4.5 CLOSE

The P3O model implementation or re-energization programme may have a long-term lifecycle or may enter a period of continual improvement supported by a performance improvement plan.

However, where a specific programme or project has been developed to set up new P3O capability, formal closure and post-implementation and benefits reviews are essential. This offers an opportunity to move from transition to making the P3O capability 'business as usual' and allows time for reflection and review – asking the question 'Was it worth it?'

External consultants or contractors who were brought in to fast-track the improvement programme may be released, as long as a full skills transfer to organization resources has been completed.

After closing the programme, it is essential to maintain the role of P3O sponsor as a champion for the P3O and maintain relationships with the key stakeholders. The P3O needs to continue to provide functions and services that are aligned with the business requirements, and it is likely that support and investment will be required for further changes to be delivered through subsequent programmes or projects.

5 Roles within a P3O model

When designing the P3O and deciding on the right model, job descriptions should be identified that are specific for each resource. The job descriptions may focus on a management role (e.g. head of programme office), a generic role (e.g. portfolio analyst), a specific function (e.g. finance officer) or a combination of different functions.

Outlines of the various roles are provided in the following sections. The role descriptions can be treated as a 'pick and mix' set to create customized job descriptions tailored to the organization's business and customer requirements.

5.1 MANAGEMENT ROLES

P3O sponsor

The P3O sponsor is a senior manager who directs and champions the establishment and evolving operation of the P3O. They will ideally be a member of the main board.

Head of P3O (permanent office)

The head of P3O (also known as head of portfolio office) establishes and runs the office.

This role requires strong leadership and management skills, coupled with strong PPM or strategy/business-planning skills, to ensure the integrity of the portfolio or programmes and projects. The individual will also provide strategic challenge, overview and scrutiny, ensuring alignment with wider policy and strategic initiatives.

In some organizations, the head of P3O may be a strategic or business-planning manager or director.

Head of programme or project office (temporary office)

The head of programme or project office establishes and runs the office and may deputize for the programme or project manager.

The role requires strong leadership and management skills, coupled with strong PPM skills, to ensure the integrity of the programme or project. The individual will also provide strategic challenge, overview and scrutiny, ensuring alignment with wider policy and strategic initiatives.

5.2 GENERIC ROLES

Portfolio analyst

This role facilitates the development and ongoing management of an optimized portfolio, ensuring senior management decisions lead to the fulfilment of strategic objectives through the delivery of programmes and projects (aligned with business-as-usual objectives).

The portfolio analyst develops and maintains management dashboards.

Programme or project specialist (internal consultant)

The specialist role provides hands-on support for programme and project managers. The individual plays a proactive role in knowledge management to promote programme and project management methods and the roll-out of best programme and project management practice. They provide a consultancy service to programme and project managers or programme and project boards, delivering hands-on assistance to support the successful delivery of the programme or project.

Programme or project officer

The purpose of the programme or project officer (also known as programme or project coordinator or administrator) is to improve the planning and delivery process by collecting and maintaining data in a consistent form. It is the responsibility of programme or project officers to implement guidelines, procedures and templates to collect and maintain this data and provide hands-on delivery support to a programme or project.

5.3 FUNCTIONAL ROLES

In a large or permanent office, the functional roles may be allocated to a single person or multiple people. In a small or temporary office, however, these roles will often be combined in a single person's job description.

Benefits and value

The benefits and value role ensures that a consistent 'fit for purpose' approach to benefits and value management is applied across the portfolio or programme and that benefits realization is optimized from the organization's investment in change.

Commercial

The commercial role ensures that the organization carries out the role of 'informed customer' and that all commercial/procurement practices and decisions meet designated standards and offer the organization value for money.

This may be a P3O role, but it is more likely to be embedded in the P3O, with formal line management from the commercial, procurement or purchasing function. It may also exist within a virtual P3O.

Communications and stakeholder engagement

The communications and stakeholder engagement role ensures that stakeholder analysis is undertaken regularly and that a communications plan is designed and implemented successfully. In high-profile P3Os this role may manage relationships with the media.

Information management

The information management role is the custodian and guardian of all master copies of the portfolio, programme or project's information. The role encompasses configuration management duties.

This role should work closely with any information assurance department or functions, as well as with those in the issue and change control roles.

Consultancy and performance management

The consultancy and performance management role provides internal consultancy and expertise in PPM and organization processes. Its services are focused on maintaining minimum standards and achieving target performance across the organization. It seeks to continually improve the performance of the portfolio, programme and projects within an organization, and also creates, maintains and disseminates good practice.

Finance

The finance role establishes a professional finance function within the portfolio, programme or project to ensure the timely provision of funding and effective financial control.

This may be a P3O role, but it is more likely to be embedded in the P3O, with formal line management from the corporate finance function.

Issue

The issue role takes the lead in ensuring that the portfolio, programme or project has effective processes in place to identify, monitor and resolve issues. It should be closely aligned with the information management and change control roles.

Change control

The change control role takes the lead in ensuring that the portfolio, programme or project has effective processes in place to identify, monitor and deliver changes. It should be closely aligned with the information management and issue roles.

Planning and estimating

The planning and estimating role is responsible for facilitating the development and maintenance of the portfolio, programme or project plan and dependency logs.

Quality assurance

The quality assurance role leads the work to ensure that the new products or services delivered by the portfolio, programme or project are fit for purpose and are capable of delivering the benefits required by the relevant board/management level.

Resource management

The resource management role ensures that current and future programmes and projects are equipped with enough staff with the right skills, at the time they are needed, and that these resources are used as efficiently as possible.

Risk

The risk role takes the lead in ensuring that the portfolio, programme or project has effective processes in place to identify and monitor risks, has access to reliable and up-to-date information about risks, and uses the appropriate controls and actions to deal with risks.

The role should ensure that all risk management practices are consistent with the corporate risk management policy and strategy. It is closely related to the issue role.

Reporting

The reporting role provides a reporting service to the portfolio, programme or project. It collates base data and generates reports to multiple audiences through aggregated data.

Secretariat/administrator

The secretariat/administrator role provides portfolio, programme or project administrative support. It may also provide a secretariat function for the relevant boards.

Tools expert

The tools expert role offers expertise in software tools to support the change environment. The role may provide support to the PPM community to configure software, or provide training and coaching in its use. Examples of tools may include enterprise programme and project software, and planning, risk, document management or collaboration tools.

Further information

For more information on AXELOS and its portfolio of guidance, including P3M3, see www.axelos.com

Relevant AXELOS guidance includes:

AXELOS (2013). *Portfolio, Programme and Project Offices* (2013). The Stationery Office, London.

Cabinet Office (2011). *Managing Successful Programmes.* The Stationery Office, London.

Office of Government Commerce (2002). *Tailoring PRINCE2.* The Stationery Office, London.

Office of Government Commerce (2009). *Directing Successful Projects with PRINCE2.* The Stationery Office, London.

Office of Government Commerce (2009). *Managing Successful Projects with PRINCE2.* The Stationery Office, London.

Office of Government Commerce (2010). *Management of Risk: Guidance for Practitioners.* The Stationery Office, London.

Office of Government Commerce (2010). *Management of Value.* The Stationery Office, London.

Office of Government Commerce (2011). *Management of Portfolios.* The Stationery Office, London.

Glossary

assurance

All the systematic actions necessary to provide confidence that the target (system, process, organization, programme, project, outcome, benefit, capability, product output, deliverable) is appropriate. Appropriateness might be defined subjectively or objectively in different circumstances. The implication is that assurance will have a level of independence from that which is being assured.

centre of excellence (COE)

A coordinating function for all or part of PPM ensuring change is delivered consistently and well, through standard processes and competent staff. It may provide standards, consistency of methods and processes, knowledge management, assurance and training. It may also provide strategic oversight, scrutiny and challenge across an organization's portfolio of programmes and projects. It may be a function within a wider scope of P3O or may be the only function of a P3O. This function provides a focal point for driving the implementation of improvements to increase the organization's capability and capacity in programme and project delivery.

chief executive officer (CEO)

Describes the role in a commercial organization with the highest level of authority for the total management of the business.

chief financial officer (CFO)

Describes the role in a commercial organization with the highest level of authority for the management of the financial risks, planning and reporting for a business. This role will generally report to the CEO.

chief information officer (CIO)

Describes the role in a commercial organization with the highest level of authority for the management of information technology for the business. This role will generally report to the CEO but may also report to the CFO in smaller organizations.

chief operating officer (COO)

Describes the role in a commercial organization with the highest level of authority for the development, design, management and improvement of the open systems that create and deliver the organization's products and/or services. This role will generally report to the CEO.

gated review

A structured review of a project, programme or portfolio as part of formal governance arrangements carried out at key decision points in the lifecycle to ensure that the decision to invest as per agreed business cases and plans remains valid.

hub and spoke

A term to describe a system of organizational design for P3O where there is a centralized office (the hub) connected (via spokes) to a number of small decentralized offices (sub-hubs) each with a subset of the centralized office's business objectives, functions and services. All information and processes (connections) are arranged so that they move along spokes to the hub at the centre. A hub-and-spoke model provides the benefit of scalability for large organizations and supports business ownership by maintaining a level of decentralization.

management dashboard

A technique to represent vast amounts of decision-support information at an amalgamated level using tabular and graphic representation such as graphs and traffic lights.

***Managing Successful Programmes* (MSP)**

An AXELOS publication/method representing proven programme management good practice in successfully delivering transformational change, drawn from the experiences of both public- and private-sector organizations. See section on further information.

organization portfolio office

A type of P3O model that is designed to centrally manage the investment process, strategic alignment, prioritization and selection, progress tracking and monitoring, optimization and benefits achieved by an organization's projects and programmes on behalf of its senior management.

P3O sponsor

A senior manager with appropriate authority who champions the establishment and evolving operation of the P3O. They will ideally be a member of the main board.

Portfolio, Programme and Project Management (PPM)

A collective term used for a series of guides aimed at improving the performance of those involved in portfolio, programme and project management. PPM is the accepted term in the industry and covers portfolio as well as programme and project management.

Portfolio, Programme and Project Management Maturity Model (P3M3)

A framework with which organizations can assess their current performance and put in place improvement plans. See section on further information.

***Portfolio, Programme and Project Offices* (P3O)**

An AXELOS publication describing the decision-enabling and support business model for all business change within an organization. This will include single or multiple physical or virtual structures, i.e. offices (permanent and/or temporary), providing a mix of central and localized functions and services, and integration with governance arrangements and the wider business such as other corporate support functions. See section on further information.

programme brief

A statement that describes the specific objectives, required benefits, potential risks, outline costs, timescales and potential options for delivery for a programme.

PRojects IN Controlled Environments (PRINCE2)

The standard UK government methodology for project management. See section on further information.

senior responsible owner (SRO)

The single individual with overall responsibility for ensuring that a project or programme meets its objectives and delivers the projected benefits.